# Praise for *At Your Fingertips!*

"Tells you how to make those paralyzing decisions about what to keep and what to throw out. Needless to say, it's a neat, well organized book."—*Vancouver Province*

"A brilliant blueprint for organizing information."
—*The Peak*, Powell River, B.C.

"The procedures and advice offered are sensible and very detailed. Most organizing books don't cover paper management thoroughly enough. This is THE definitive book on paper management. Highly recommended!"—Judy Brown, professional organizer

"You are my patron saint of organizing! When I received your information I almost cried . . . As you can guess, I was feeling pretty overwhelmed."—Jan, Surrey, B.C.

"I knew this system would work because you had a place for coupons and take-out menus!"—Irene, Abbotsford, B.C.

"Alexandra (Sandie) Bradley and her former student Denise Dale have endeared themselves to the reading public with *At Your Fingertips! A Household Filing System That Works for You.*"
—Rebecca Wigod, *Vancouver Sun*

"Do you recall the TV program *The Avengers?* . . . Meet *The Organizers!* Denise and Alexandra are whizzes at getting information under control."—Robert Chesterman, *West Coast Editor*

"I really love the system and use it religiously. Our busy family couldn't do without it!!"—Tanyce Westgard, Surrey, B.C.

Also available from

STREAMLINE BOOKS

*At Your Fingertips in the Office:*
*Information Management for the*
*Small Business*

# At Your
# FINGERTIPS!

## A Household Filing System
## That Works for You

Denise Dale and Alexandra Bradley

Second edition 2004

04 05 06 07 08    5 4 3 2 1

Streamline Information and Organizing Services
186 – 8210 No. 2 Road, Suite #271
Richmond, British Columbia
Canada  V7C 2V4
www.streamlinebooks.com

**National Library of Canada**
**Cataloguing in Publication**

Dale, Denise, 1961–
    At your fingertips! : a household filing system that works for you / Denise Dale and Alexandra Bradley ; Paper Trail Publishing, editing. —2nd ed.

Includes bibliographical references and index.
ISBN 0-9685727-2-3

    1. Filing systems.  2. Family records—Management.
I. Bradley, Alexandra, 1948–  II. Title.

TX326.D34 2004        640        C2004-901382-3


A catalog record for this book is available from the Library of Congress.

Editing: Paper Trail Publishing
Design: Carty Design (first edition)
Cover design: Leon Phillips (second edition)
Printed in Canada by Friesens

**To our families:**
Don, Aaron, Wesley and Diana Dale,
who made the household filing system a necessity and a success,
and Eric, Karen and Steve Bradley,
who have patiently endured quick dinners and prototypes
to see this project come to pass

# Contents

# Introduction

*At Your Fingertips!* WILL HELP YOU GET ORGANIZED BY SHOWING you a system that keeps track of personal schedules, information and papers. It will help you decide what to keep, where to put it and for how long and give you the reasons why. By organizing your personal information and papers you will save your household time, money and stress.

Ask yourself the following questions:
- Can you find your birth certificate?
- Do you know where your passport is?
- Do you know how long you should keep telephone bills and utility statements?
- Have you ever turned the house upside down looking for an important piece of paper—like a child's permission slip to go on a field trip to the pumpkin patch?
- Do you know how long you should keep credit card receipts? Where should you keep them?

Once upon a time most of us did not have trouble keeping track of our birth certificate or where we had stashed the utility statement. We did not have trouble popping documents into a couple of file folders, whether electronic or paper. The process used to be quite simple, until the number of people, pets and things in our households started to grow, and the word "schedule" became synonymous with the phrases "juggling act," "tag-team parenting" or "sandwich generation." Or perhaps simply the passage of time has witnessed a few paper piles grow into a now out-of-control mess!

Years ago, all of a household's important papers could fit quite nicely in a single briefcase. This just does not seem to be the case today. Consider the mail. As one records organizer has observed, we receive more mail in a week than our parents did in a month. We receive, in a month, more mail than our grandparents did in a year.

As you join together to form a family, and as that family grows, your "simple" filing system or the drawer you have set aside "for papers" does not seem to work as well as it did. You cannot find anything, and you do not know what you have. Furthermore, you might not be able to decide what to keep, where to put it and for how long or know the reasons why.

Some people cope with information overload by simply throwing everything away. Others hang on to every scrap of information that comes their way, "just in case" they need it some day. Between pitching and hoarding there is a balanced process by which organization, control and rational decision-making dictate what information should be kept, where, for how long and why. *At Your Fingertips!* can help you achieve this balanced process.

## Save Time

Experts suggest you need to take a look at how you are organizing information if you cannot find a needed document in five minutes or less. How much time do you spend shuffling piles of paper around the house? Think of all those crazy mornings spent trying to find papers before the school bus pulled up to the drive. Think of all those Saturday afternoons you spent looking for those expensive concert tickets tucked away in a safe spot (so safe you could not remember where it was!). Once you realize just how much time you spend looking for papers and information, you will appreciate and enjoy the extra time you gain by becoming organized. You know you will indeed be able to locate (and, in most cases, physically go and get) a document or the information you need in five minutes or less.

**Save Money**

Most people want to save money. Once you are organized, you will avoid late charges on bills and other fines. Even small fines (for example, overdue charges of 25 cents per day per book at the library) accumulate quickly. Bills can get paid on time—whether by phone, by mail, over the Internet or in person—because you know where they are, when they are due and have a system in place for making sure they get paid on time. Now you will be reminded that the school play starts at 5:30 p.m. and you will be able to plan ahead for a quick, simple dinner instead of rushing out and spending money on fast food. You will also save money on stationery supplies, cabinets, bookshelves and other organizing products, because chances are you will not have that much to store anymore.

**Save Space**

Information can take up a lot of space. When you streamline the amount of paper and information you keep, you save space—whether it is in your home or on your computer. Think of how much space you'll recover when you finally have the courage and know-how to tackle those growing piles of paper scattered around the house and to remove what you know you do not need.

### Avoid Frustration and Stress

Personal information management gone awry can cause frustration and stress. Maybe you already know what it is like to tear your house apart looking for a misplaced piece of paper or an important document. Maybe it was a case of trying to find a child's permission slip for the class field trip (which was that same morning!) while a carpool parent was out front, leaning on the horn. Maybe it was a case of you starting off the family vacation by tearing apart the house looking for your passport while the rest of the family headed off to the airport—without you! If your papers are properly organized, you can circumvent such stressful scenarios.

### Avoid Personal Embarrassment

Imagine showing up for dinner at your boss's house a day early because you misplaced the invitation but were "sure" about the date. Or going to the library to check out books, only to discover that you have lost one and have two checked out already that are now overdue. Add to this embarrassment a fines total that grows daily. Think of the time spent looking for the lost book and the frustration of waiting in line to straighten everything out at the fines counter.

A lot of us, if we sat and thought about it for a moment, could come up with our own examples of how mismanagement of personal information and papers has caused us grief. Can this book really help? Yes. Having a system in place to help you organize and properly manage your personal information, schedules and papers can help you simplify and streamline your life.

Before you go on, keep in mind that *At Your Fingertips!* is for personal household use only. It does not take into account any activities or regulations associated with home-based business activity. Also, it is a suggested model only. Modify it to suit your own needs. If you find that you disagree with a suggestion or guideline, make a note to yourself to change the system to reflect your own decisions, ideas, preferences or habits. The beauty of this system is that it will encourage you to sit down and think about your method of personal information and records management. Once you have completed the process described here and have set up a filing system that is appropriate for you and your family, making it work and having it work for you is simply a matter of routine, day-to-day use and maintenance.

# 1

# What to Keep?

*Making Decisions*

WHAT PERSONAL OR HOUSEHOLD PAPERS AND INFORMATION YOU choose to keep depends upon your circumstances. There are very few laws or regulations that dictate how long you or your family must keep and be able to produce certain information. For example, if you earn income, you must file an income tax return and keep a copy of it according to applicable government regulations. Also, you may be keeping some documents because your lawyer, accountant or financial planner has suggested you do so.

Beyond having to keep some information for legal reasons, what you keep is really up to you. This is one reason so many of us feel confused (or even at a complete loss) when it comes to taking care of our personal papers and information. It *is* up to us—and we are not sure what to do about it.

The information you should keep hinges on your personal decisions about what information or documents best fulfill the needs of you and your household. What documents do you need to provide proof of ownership or identity? What documents do you need to keep the household running smoothly? One thing is certain: what you decide to keep and what you decide to toss out will differ from what the people next door, your friends or your relatives choose to keep.

One of the keys to getting family papers and information under control is to look at the big picture—at not just your present needs, but your future needs as well. Take the time to make decisions that will serve as guidelines for many years to come. To help make those decisions, look at the "Household Filing System at a Glance" (see pages 24–25) and think about adopting the system as is or modifying it to suit your needs.

You will want to consider keeping all information that affects the daily running of your home. Some items, like schedules, appointment information or phone numbers, need only be kept for a short period of time, for they are constantly changing. Usually, this is the type of information you will want to keep at your fingertips. Other information, while perhaps not needed on a frequent basis, needs to be kept for a longer or indefinite period of time. Finally, some information reflects personal interests and reference needs—this, too, can be useful but may have a limited life. What you hear or read about from experts in the areas of law, finances or even family history may also help you modify the system to suit your own needs.

Finally, sit back and think about the circumstances in which you might want to keep information. Take the time to reflect and make decisions. The following questions are some you might ask yourself when deciding whether or not to keep information.

*Do I need this information?*
- for legal purposes?
- for income tax purposes?
- to establish ownership?
- to establish identity?
- to document achievements?
- for sentimental purposes?
- for the family archives?

*Who originated this information?*
- Are they keeping copies of the information, too?

*Where else can I get this information?*
- From the original source?
- From the library?

*How much of a certain kind of information is "enough"?*
- Do I want to keep *all* my child's schoolwork?
- Do I want to keep *only samples* of my child's schoolwork?

You may be trying to organize and keep track of a lot information that you do not really need to keep in the first place. You are not the local newspaper clipping service, and you are not the public library. As a matter of fact, the library is a good place to turn to for information such as newspaper and magazine articles or newsletters. Keep in mind that organizations that issue newsletters likely will have a copy of every one published. You could probably request a copy should you ever need it. Even items such as credit card receipts can usually be retrieved from the credit card company (although sometimes at a price).

If you have difficulty tossing out information, tell yourself that the less information you collect, the less information you will have to organize and maintain. According to professional records managers, 80 to 85 percent of paper collected is never looked at again. Although this sobering statistic is based on the business office, it is worth keeping in mind if your household seems to collect more than its fair share of information. Know your reasons and make your decisions accordingly.

Information you choose to keep is best organized in files. The next chapter suggests a system for organizing your information and provides more specifics on what documents you might want to keep.

# 2
# Where to Put It?
*Getting Organized*

ONCE YOU HAVE DECIDED WHAT TO KEEP, YOU WILL NEED TO decide where to put it. Paper and electronic information is best kept in organized files or containers. But before you break open that new package of file folders or CDs, take a step back and think about how you want to organize your information. What sort of logic will help you find information once you have put it away?

The household filing system described in this book divides information into four general categories:

Fingertip Files

Household Files

Permanent Files

Reference Files

Dividing your information into these four distinct categories not only helps you to keep it organized, but it also helps you to make decisions about *how long to keep* information. Here is a quick look at the purpose behind each of the categories, some examples of what you might find in them and a brief description of how they should be organized. Further details about what to keep in each category can be found in the next chapter.

## Fingertip Files

 These files contain information you need to grab in a hurry. This could include calendar and appointment information, current newsletters, telephone numbers, business cards, class lists, tickets, financial transaction receipts, schedules—any kind of information you need to sort for quick retrieval as you head out the door, pay the bills or make a quick phone call. Most information stored in the Fingertip Files will be temporary in nature and constantly changing. Once you have finished with the information, you can discard it.

Never again hunt for misplaced theater tickets while the babysitter looks on. Never again forget to send your child to preschool in pajamas for Pajama Day. Never again have to phone directory assistance for misplaced telephone numbers. Now you will have this information and more right at your fingertips.

Keep this information near the "information center" in your home. For many families this is somewhere in the kitchen near the phone. A set of three-ring binders works well for keeping track of this information. (For more information on the setup of these files, see Appendix A.)

### How to Organize Fingertip Files

Start by dividing the Fingertip Files into three broad subject areas. You can expand or condense the number of categories to suit the needs of your household, but suggested here are:

Calendar
Contacts/Schedules/Newsletters
Shopping/Family Business

The *Calendar* category is exactly that—a system based on calendar dates to keep track of appointments, commitments and things to do. The calendar allows you to file date-sensitive information and papers by date for retrieval as they are needed. Examples include:

Bills to Pay
Claim Stubs (dry-cleaning, appliances, shoe or watch repair)
Library Receipts
Permission Slips
Tickets

The *Contacts/Schedules/Newsletters* category is also self-explanatory. Here you can keep phone numbers, the condo membership list, business cards, the daycare friendship list, minutes from the daycare parents' meeting, the pool schedule, the weekly school newsletter, the garbage schedule, the recycling schedule/information, information for the babysitter, and so on. Examples include:

Addresses
Business Cards
Newsletters
Phone Numbers
Schedules

The *Shopping/Family Business* category is where you can keep track of day-to-day financial papers, such as bank receipts, store receipts and credit card receipts, and information you want to keep close at hand, such as take-out menus or coupons (if you use them). Examples of information to include here are:

Receipts for Groceries
Banking Receipts
Coupons and Offers
Credit Card Receipts
Merchandise Receipts
Service Receipts
Take-Out Menus

Three categories are generally enough—but you might want or need to have one or two more depending on the needs of your family. Although information in the Fingertip Files is generally temporary in nature, you might want to transfer a small number of documents and receipts into one of the other files (Household, Permanent or Reference) after the immediate need for them has passed.

In one large Canadian city there was a rash of burglaries all linked to a dumpster behind an insurance company. An enterprising thief discovered expired insurance documents in the dumpster and proceeded to make out his "shopping list." To protect yourself from fraud and theft, you should shred or destroy beyond recognition all papers containing personal information such as your name, address, credit card numbers or bank account information.

You should also question "routine" requests for your personal information. The next time you are at a cash desk and the clerk wants to enter your telephone number into the computer, ask why this is necessary. Try to ensure that companies keeping information about you use it and dispose of it in an appropriate way and in compliance with privacy regulations. The next time you renew your house insurance, ask the insurance representative to identify those who have access to your personal information and to describe how your information is used, stored and disposed of. Ask if the organization has a formal privacy protection code.

## Household Files

These files contain information necessary in the administration of your life and home. They include information and documents related to finances, utilities, education, employment, extracurricular activities and warranties. This kind of information will be needed for a longer period than the Fingertip Files and may eventually be transferred to the Permanent Files.

### How to Organize Household Files

The key here is to identify groupings or topics that simplify your job of putting the paper away. Household

Files should probably include items from the following list of categories:

Automobile

Budget

Child Care

Contracts

Education

Employment

Extracurricular Activities

Family and Friends

Finances

Health

Home

Insurance

Investments

Memberships

Pets

Subscriptions

Tax

Travel

Utilities

Warranties and Instructions

Using broad subject groupings will make it easy to locate and file information. Subdivide these into as many detailed categories as you need. Filing by subject or topic makes it easier to retrieve all files associated with a specific household function. For example, if you want to arrange for a loan to clear off some credit card debt, it is easier to retrieve all the relevant files if they are located together in one or two categories than it is to hunt through your entire filing system looking for information. Keeping your relevant files together can also help to ensure that needed files are not accidentally missed.

Keep logical groupings in alphabetical order. For example, you might have information for the following categories:

Cable

Electricity

Natural Gas

Telephone

Water and Sewer

These categories could be grouped together under the umbrella heading of Utilities, as shown.

Utilities: Cable

Utilities: Electricity

Utilities: Natural Gas

Utilities: Telephone: Cellular service

Local service

Long-distance service

Utilities: Water and Sewer

You will need to set up some file folders or containers in which to store your Household Files. A kitchen drawer works well for storing the files, particularly if it is located near the information hub in your home. If you do not have a spare drawer, there are lots of alternatives available. Consider using a cardboard box designed for file folders, often referred to as a "banker's box," or a tote file box with a handle, which makes it easier to move the box from closet to kitchen table. If you typically do not have a lot of information to collect, you could also consider setting up your files in binders. (See Appendix A for setup instructions.)

When organizing your files, always make it easy to put something away in the right spot, even if that means taking an extra minute to find something in a particular file. In other words, do not make your file headings so detailed that finding the right place to file something becomes a chore. For example, consider keeping insurance papers for all your cars together in one file rather than breaking them down into individual files for each car. Consider how often you access that information, how much information is actually stored there, and keep it simple. Functionality should win out over aesthetics here—you want to get your system up and running. You might want to keep a master copy of your Household Files list of categories as the first item in your filing cabinet, drawer or box. Keep the papers in their categories by date order: oldest on the bottom, newest on the top.

| Tip: Keep Digital and Paper Files Consistent | If you use a computer to keep records, set up your file folders on your computer to mirror your paper files. This will help you retrieve information quickly. A notation such as "*" or "E" could be used on your paper file folders to identify information that is also located on your computer. |

# Permanent Files

These files contain information that establishes identity  and proves ownership as well as information to be kept for sentimental or genealogical purposes. This includes birth, marriage or death certificates, military papers, personal and family memorabilia, education records, household inventory, wills and property records. This kind of information is required or desired to be kept for a very long period of time, perhaps even beyond our own lifetimes, to be passed on to future generations.

Vital records, genealogical (family history) papers, sentimental items and information that we are required by law to keep for a long period of time (such as wills, deeds and income tax returns), should be kept together in an area designed for Permanent Files. Records related to the family or having genealogical or sentimental value preserve the memory or story of the family. Vital records are important for genealogical purposes, however, their more immediate value is that they establish our identities, provide proof of ownership, provide evidence of legal agreements, establish our credentials, and so on.

## How to Organize Permanent Files
Permanent Files can include:

> Certificates (birth, death, marriage)
> Citizenship/Immigration Records
> Divorce Decree/Custody Agreements
> Education Records (Diplomas, Transcripts)
> Health Records
> Memorabilia/Family Archives
> Military Records

Personal Property/Inventory Records

Property Records (Deeds)

Religious Documents (Baptism Records)

Social Security/Social Insurance Documents

Tax Documents

Travel Documents

Voter Identification Cards

Wills

As with the Household Files, you will want to prepare file folders for each category. Alternatively, you may want to set up files for each person in your household using these categories as subdivisions under the person's name (for example, Child #1: Certificates; Child #1: Education Records). We intend to keep permanent records for a long time, perhaps to bequeath them to our children. Where and how we store this information becomes important, because original documents can be difficult, if not impossible, to replace. If this information is important to you, keep it in a secure spot, such as a fireproof file container, a safe or a safety deposit box, or in the care of a reputable off-site storage facility that specializes in the care of information.

If you want to keep some of this information (or copies of some of it) in your home for easy reference, consider storing it in archival-quality containers and file folders that can help preserve and extend the life of documents. Archival-quality containers and folders are available in a variety of sizes, making the storage of oversize documents easier. The information should be kept in a room with appropriate humidity and temperature. The best place is one where you feel most comfortable, such as the main living area of your house.

Permanent documents are important. Generally, the environment in a basement or attic is too extreme for paper and could cause your records to deteriorate.

Many off-site storage facilities offer a file retrieval and delivery service for a modest fee. These facilities are sometimes listed in the Yellow Pages of your telephone directory under headings such as "Office Records Stored" or "Storage—Office Records."

| Use colored file folders to visually distinguish your file categories (for example, red for household files, blue for permanent files, yellow for reference files). | **Tip: Color Your Files** |
|---|---|

## Reference Files

These files contain information of interest to you but that may not be necessary in the administration of your life and home. This information could include newspaper and magazine clippings, handouts, brochures about topics of personal interest such as gardening, maps, recipes to try or home improvement ideas. This kind of information often ends up as miscellaneous piles around the house. Usually you keep this information because you think you are going to read it again.

Reference Files are files where you can store any "outside" information you come across, such as ideas for birthday parties or travel brochures. Here you might keep, perhaps at whim, information of interest to you or members of your household. Because this information relates more to personal interest than to specific household requirements, it does not usually hold the same value as the Household or Permanent Files.

## How to Organize Reference Files

Reference Files can include subject information or items such as the following:

Books

Calendars/Course Information

Catalogs (mail-order, retail)

Computers

Crafts

Entertainment

Garden

Gift Ideas

Instructions

Parenting

Recipes

Travel

As with the Household and Permanent Files, set up file folders for each category. The type of information you keep may vary quite a bit from this list. Use titles that are meaningful to you; this will allow you to quickly identify the folder in which you have placed information and to later retrieve it. A reminder: much of the information stored here (such as newspaper clippings) will become outdated quickly and can be obtained from other sources. Don't let information accumulate here.

Keep what you want in the Reference Files, but put a date on the information. The date will come in handy later when you go through your files in an annual purge. Anything you have not used in two years or more should probably be tossed, because this is an area where clutter can really pile up, especially if you are a "keeper."

**Tip:
Date Your
Files**

Once you have decided upon how you will organize your files, you must put all your papers away. But first, relax, and don't feel overwhelmed. If you've followed us this far, you will have four distinct groups of files. Take a breather, make out your list of supplies and then go ahead and create some files. The following chart shows how the whole system comes together. The next chapter provides suggestions for how long you should keep files and why.

# Household Filing System

**Fingertip Files**

*Calendar*
  - Bills to Pay
  - Claim Slips
  - Library Receipts
  - Permission Slips
  - Tickets

*Contacts/Schedules/Newsletters*
  - Addresses
  - Business Cards
  - Newsletters
  - Phone Numbers
  - Schedules

*Shopping/Family Business*
  - Receipts for Groceries
  - Banking Receipts
  - Coupons and Offers
  - Credit Card Receipts
  - Merchandise Receipts
  - Service Receipts
  - Take-Out Menus

**Household Files**

  - Automobile
  - Budget
  - Child Care
  - Contracts
  - Education
  - Employment
  - Extracurricular Activities
  - Family and Friends
  - Finances
  - Health
  - Home
  - Insurance
  - Investments
  - Memberships
  - Pets
  - Subscriptions
  - Tax
  - Travel
  - Utilities
  - Warranties and Instructions

# at a Glance

**Permanent Files**

Certificates
Citizenship/Immigration Records
Divorce Decree/Custody Agreements
Education Records
Health Records
Memorabilia/Family Archives
Military Records
Personal Property/Inventory Records
Property Records
Religious Documents
Social Security/Social Insurance Documents
Tax Documents
Travel Documents
Voter Identification Cards
Wills

**Reference Files**

Books
Calendars/Course Information
Catalogs
Computers
Crafts
Entertainment
Garden
Gift Ideas
Instructions
Parenting
Recipes
Travel

# 3
# For How Long and Why?

*Retention Guidelines*

To help you decide how long to keep documents, in this chapter we share our suggested guidelines and the reasons behind them. These are reasons based on personal experience, information from government officials and businesses, and common sense. Use this book as a workbook. By all means, if your reasons differ from ours, note them, then change the guidelines to reflect your personal situation. The key to streamlining your information is to think about how you will use the information being kept and ultimately to come up with your own personal response to the question: Why am I keeping it?

The guidelines on the following pages are arranged according to the four broad categories already discussed: Fingertip Files, Household Files, Permanent Files and Reference Files. Note that "Selectively retain" means to retain *some* records permanently. This means you should to go through the documents in your file and choose the ones you feel are worth saving. Then transfer these "keepers" to the Permanent Files. *Toss the rest!* (You will probably apply "Selectively retain" quite often to children's schoolwork.)

| | |
|---|---|
| If you find yourself involved in a dispute about a particular matter, suspend the retention guidelines governing that topic. Keep everything pertaining to the dispute, regardless of what the guidelines suggest, until the matter has been resolved. | **Tip:** <br> **Be Flexible** |

# Fingertip Files

## Calendar

*Discard after use*

Items kept here provide information or documents needed on a specific day. The information is then appropriately distributed or discarded after use.

Examples of distributed information:
- credit card statement—once paid, it is put into the Household Files under "Finances: Credit Card"
- signed permission slip—routed to child's school
- theater tickets—handed to the usher for admission
- tickets to child's university graduation ceremony—once used, the tickets might be kept for sentimental reasons. They should be put into the Household Files under "Family and Friends: Memorabilia." (On your annual purge, they might be transferred to the Permanent Files.)

Examples of information discarded immediately after use:
- instructions regarding an event such as a child's field trip
- list of things to do
- time and location of an auction advertised in the paper. (Once you have arrived at your destination, there is no need to keep the information any longer.)

## Contacts

*Current only*

Replace or revise this information once you receive more current information. Phone lists, individual phone numbers, addresses, business cards, class or club lists, and so on are used to make contact with people or businesses. Outdated phone numbers and addresses cannot do that for you, so get rid of them.

If you ever need to find an old address (perhaps you need to track where a relative lived for genealogical purposes), you might be able to get the information from libraries, which often have city directories, "criss-cross" directories (arranged by address) and phone books from previous years. If your neighborhood library does not have these materials, ask for help from the librarian, who can be a mine of information.

**Tip: Finding an Old Address**

### Schedules
*Current only*

Schedules for garbage collection/recycling, recreation centers and meetings should be replaced when new ones are received. Outdated schedules usually have outdated information. Get rid of them!

If you ever need to refer to an old schedule, check with the organization that originally produced it. Chances are they will have a copy on file or in their archives.

**Tip: Go to the Source**

### Newsletters
*Current only*

Replace existing newsletters from schools, clubs and other organizations of interest when new ones are received. Newsletters provide the latest news from or updated information about an organization, its activities and members. They can also provide related information of interest to members. Keep the current one handy for access to the latest news and events. If there is information in the newsletter that you want to keep once a newer one has arrived, file it in an appropriate place. For example, a new telephone number for a member should be added or updated in **Contacts** in the Fingertip Files. If you must keep some back issues of newsletters, file them in the Household Files under an appropriate category, such as "Memberships: (Name of Organization)" or "Education: (Name of School)."

### Shopping/Family Business
*Current only*

| | |
|---|---|
| Receipts for groceries | *Keep only if used for budgeting* |
| Bank transaction receipts | *Until verified by statement* |
| Coupons and offers | *Until expiry date* |
| Credit card receipts | *Until verified by statement* |
| Major purchase receipts | *14 days from purchase or as per stated return policy, then transfer to the Household Files* |
| Minor purchase receipts | *14 days from purchase or as per stated return policy* |
| Service receipts | *As stated on receipt* |

Bank receipts need only be kept until an updated bank statement or passbook can verify them. Often bank statements will outline their policy, which is usually that if the statement is not disputed within 30 days, it will become the official record. If in doubt about your bank's policy, check with them.

Credit card receipts usually need only be kept until you have received your monthly statement. Once you have verified the transaction on your statement as correct, there is no need to keep the receipts. They can be destroyed. If for some reason you later discover that you need a copy of the receipt, it is often possible to obtain a copy from the credit card company. Review your statements or initial credit application correspondence and brochures to determine policies. One credit card company states clearly on the reverse of its monthly statements that replacement statements are available at a charge of two dollars and that copies of receipts are available for three dollars.

Receipts for major purchases that might be needed for insurance purposes should be kept here for the duration of the stated return policy, then transferred to either the Household Files and filed under "Home: Personal Property/Inventory" or kept with the Permanent Files and filed under "Personal Property Records." Note: in most cases it is the merchant or store receipt rather than the credit card receipt that is needed for insurance purposes. Receipts for routine or minor purchases need only be kept for the duration of the seller's stated return policy. In many cases this is a standard 14- or 30-day return policy.

## Household Files

Most of the information in the Household Files will be discarded after about 18 months to several years. Information of vital importance or that needs to be kept for a longer period of time should be transferred to the Permanent Files.

### Automobile

Keep here correspondence and all other documents about or receipts for major repairs, gas and maintenance for each car.

| | |
|---|---|
| Correspondence | *Until auto sold* |
| Gas | *Current year only* |
| Major repairs | *Until auto sold* |
| Routine maintenance | *Until auto sold* |
| Warranty information | *Until expired* |

Correspondence and documentation about repairs, recalls or maintenance should be kept until the car is no longer owned. This documentation is also important because it shows a prospective buyer the car's history and shows that it has been properly maintained. If you find you are missing some maintenance or repair documentation, you should be able to get copies of the documents from the company that did the servicing.

Many people keep information about mileage and fuel expenses for budgeting purposes or for monitoring the performance of their car. Once a budget is revised, there is no need to keep the information any longer. Rather than keeping all documentation, jotting down summary notes on the inside of the file folder may allow you to compare average mileage from year to year. Warranty information, once it has expired, is usually of no use to you. Discard it.

## Budget
*Current year plus one*

Keep here the family budget and related "progress reports." Detailed documents outlining or projecting household expenditures need only be kept for the duration of the current budget. Once a new one has been established, you can throw the old information out. Some people might like to keep this rather revealing document. If so, transfer it to the Permanent Files under "Memorabilia/Family Archives." An alternative is to keep a summary sheet that shows the revisions over the years.

## Child Care
Keep here information, contracts and receipts relating to child care, after-school care and babysitting.

| Babysitting: | Receipts | *Current year plus one* |
|---|---|---|
| Daycare: | Contract | *Until expired* |
| | General Information | *Until superseded* |
| | Receipts | *Current year plus one* |

Keep general information about daycare, after-school care and babysitting services until the information is updated (that is, until a new daycare handbook is received) or no longer needed. Only a current contract is needed. Contracts that have been revised or have expired should only be kept until the new one is received. Receipts from daycare, child care and babysitting should be kept for the current and previous year. This guideline is to ensure that you have all the receipts needed from the previous year to claim child care expenses at income tax time. Copies of the receipts (or the originals, if not needed to accompany the filed form) used to claim a tax deduction should be transferred to a file containing a copy of your tax return and supporting documentation, filed under "Tax: Income (Year)."

### Contracts

Keep here contracts and related documents about services such as home repair, house cleaning and yard maintenance.

| | |
|---|---|
| Cleaning Service | *Until expired/superseded* |
| Home Repair | *Until expired/superseded* |
| Yard Service | *Until expired/superseded* |

Keep contracts related to the servicing of your home and possessions only as long as they are valid. Once a contract has expired or been terminated, there is no need to keep it unless you are continuing with the service and are waiting for an updated document.

### Education

Keep here all documents about education including grade school, high school, college, university, vocational institutions, night school or other continuing education. Documents to be kept could include correspondence, handbooks, course information, course work and transcripts or report cards. Once a year transfer information like report cards and samples of schoolwork that are to be kept permanently to the Permanent Files. In some cases course work supporting a postsecondary degree might be necessary as background for continuing studies or for reference support on the job; this should also be kept permanently.

| Adult #1 | Achievements/Marks | *Permanent* |
|---|---|---|
| | School/Institution: Course Work | *Selectively retain* |
| | School/Institution: General | *Selectively retain* |
| Child #1 | Records/Report Cards | *Permanent* |
| | School/Institution: General | *Current year only* |
| | School/Institution: Schoolwork | *Selectively retain* |
| Child #2 | Records/Report Cards | *Permanent* |
| | School/Institution: General | *Current year only* |
| | School/Institution: Schoolwork | *Selectively retain* |

General information about an educational institution, its policies or calendar need only be kept for the current year. Usually this type of information is updated annually by the institution, and those that it affects are given revised copies. For example, some elementary schools send home a school handbook at the start of the school year. It is necessary to keep only the current one.

Correspondence documenting achievements, such as acceptance into a university program, or important information needed during the duration of study (such as a student number) should be selectively kept, mostly to document achievements for employment purposes, admittance to additional educational programs and sentimental or genealogical purposes.

General information issued from specific instructors, departments or faculties pertaining to current courses needs to be kept only for the duration of the course. Report cards and transcripts need to be kept until the next level of achievement is reached. However, most people recognize the sentimental or genealogical value of these documents and keep them permanently. Some people consider records about course work as permanent, both for personal and business purposes. Others may choose to selectively retain some of the more outstanding samples of their work and discard the rest.

A recommendation is to keep postsecondary course notes, books and course work for a set period of time (for example, five years past the course date), then to go through all the material and selectively keep information of value to you. Keep in mind that a lot of course notes and related texts become outdated as technology, research and current events continue to change the world around us. If ever needed, updated information on course subjects will be available through libraries, educational institutions or other organizations.

## Employment

Keep here all documents about employment, including current résumé, employment history, correspondence, contracts, benefit handbooks and information about the employer/company for each working member of the household.

| | |
|---|---|
| Benefits | *Until expired* |
| Contracts | *Until expired* |
| Employer: General Correspondence | *Current year plus one* |
| Employment History | *Until superseded* |
| Handbooks | *Until superseded* |
| Résumé | *Until superseded* |

As a rule of thumb, keep general or routine correspondence between you and your employer for 12 months. Businesses typically keep routine information for two years (the current year plus one). The more time has passed since the action, the less likely the information will be needed. Keep only current employee handbooks, procedure books, benefit or contract information. If materials are expired or out-of-date, then the information they contain may be incorrect. Using incorrect information could have you operating under incorrect assumptions.

Keep copies of your current résumé or work history on hand. As you update these, throw out the old copies. It is embarrassing and unproductive to accidentally send out an outdated résumé that might not accurately reflect your education, skills, employment situation or contact information. Retain pension or benefits information until the expiry of your entitlements.

| Consider transferring one copy of your old résumé to your Permanent Files to document your employment history and achievements. Throw out any other outdated résumés. | **Tip: Updating Your Résumé?** |
|---|---|

### Extracurricular Activities

Keep here background and registration information about extracurricular activities and personal achievements. Documents could include organizational handbooks and program information, licences and achievement records. (Note: contact or member lists and meeting schedules should be kept in the Fingertip Files for quick reference.) Once a year transfer pertinent information to the Permanent Files.

| Clubs | Boy Scouts: | Achievements | *Selectively retain* |
|---|---|---|---|
| | | General Information | *Current year only* |
| | Girl Guides: | Achievements | *Selectively retain* |
| | | General Information | *Current year only* |
| | Quilters' Club: | General Information | *Current year only* |
| | Stamp Club: | General Information | *Current year only* |
| Lessons | Swimming: | Records | *Selectively retain* |
| | Skating: | Records | *Selectively retain* |
| Sports | Fishing: | Licences | *Until expired* |
| Teams | Child #1 | (Soccer) | *Current year only* |
| | Child #2 | (Swimming) | *Current year only* |

General information about extracurricular activities need only be kept for the current year or, if applicable, for as long as you or your family is involved in a particular activity. This information might include organizational handbooks, registration information, explanation of membership privileges, and so on. Annual licences, such as fishing licences or annual membership cards, and reg-istration information need only be kept until expired. Selectively keep any achievements or special honours received either as proof of status, for their value as memorabilia or for genealogical purposes. For example, a child's record of passing their first set of swimming lessons might be kept for sentimental purposes, with subsequent records kept only until the next level has been achieved. Certifications should be maintained until expiry.

## Family and Friends

Keep here general information collected about family and friends. This includes correspondence, Christmas card lists, facts such as birth dates and memorabilia. Once a year transfer information that is to be kept indefinitely to the Permanent Files under "Memorabilia."

| Birthdays | | | *Update as needed* |
|---|---|---|---|
| Correspondence | | | *Selectively retain* |
| Family History | | | *Selectively retain* |
| Family Members | Adult #1: | General | *Current year plus one* |
| | | Memorabilia | *Selectively retain* |
| | Adult #2: | General | *Current year plus one* |
| | | Memorabilia | *Selectively retain* |
| | Child #1: | General | *Current year plus one* |
| | | Memorabilia | *Selectively retain* |
| | Child #2: | General | *Current year plus one* |
| | | Memorabilia | *Selectively retain* |
| | Child #3: | General | *Current year plus one* |
| | | Memorabilia | *Selectively retain* |
| Names and Addresses | | | *Until superseded* |

This category provides a convenient spot in which to keep correspondence from friends and family and to update necessary information such as anniversaries or birth dates. Under "Names and Addresses" and "Birthdays," update as often as necessary and discard outdated information. It is a good idea to selectively keep correspondence from family and friends. Items such as annual Christmas cards might be kept until the next year—they might prove useful for updating your Christmas card list. But unless they contain a special letter, many of them could simply be enjoyed during the festive season in which they are received, then tossed out or recycled. As fewer and fewer of us write letters, much of the correspondence we do receive—either official business correspondence or personal—might be worth keeping for future generations. If you are an electronic mail user, you might want to print messages and then selectively retain them.

Under the category "Family Members (Name): General," a workable practice is to keep information for the current year plus one. After that, if it is general and routine information, throw it out. Under the subcategory "Memorabilia," you can put ticket stubs from a very special event or a program that has the name of a friend in it. Every so often go through the file and toss out what you decide really is not worth keeping. If you decide it is worth keeping, then it is probably worth the trouble to either put the item in with the Permanent Files or put it in a scrapbook so you can take it out from time to time and enjoy it. Better yet, preserve this information for years to come in archival-quality folders and containers. Reserve a special bookshelf or closet space for these items.

## Finances

Keep here correspondence and records related to banking, credit cards, employment income, loans, mortgages and pensions. (Note: in this filing system, documents related to investments and investment income are kept separately under the file heading "Investments." If you prefer, you could file investment documents here under the file name: "Finances: Investments.")

| Bank Accounts | | | |
|---|---|---|---|
| | Adult #1: | Checking | *Current year plus six* |
| | | Savings | *Current year plus six* |
| | Adult #2: | Checking | *Current year plus six* |
| | | Savings | *Current year plus six* |
| | Child #1 | | *Current year plus six* |
| | Child #2 | | *Current year plus six* |
| | Child #3 | | *Current year plus six* |

| Credit Cards | | | |
|---|---|---|---|
| | All-Purpose: | Correspondence | *Current year only* |
| | | General Information | *Current year only* |
| | | Statements | *Current year plus one* |
| | Gas Card: | Correspondence | *Current year only* |
| | | General Information | *Current year only* |
| | | Statements | *Current year plus one* |
| | Store Card: | Correspondence | *Current year only* |
| | | General Information | *Current year only* |
| | | Statements | *Current year plus one* |

| Employment Income | | | |
|---|---|---|---|
| | Employer #1: | Pay Stubs | *Current year plus one* |
| | Employer #2: | Pay Stubs | *Current year plus one* |

| Loans | | |
|---|---|---|
| | Car | *Until discharged* |
| | Personal | *Until discharged* |

| Mortgages | | |
|---|---|---|
| | First | *Until discharged* |
| | Second | *Until discharged* |

| Pension Plans | *Permanent* |
|---|---|

Financial statements, except those issued for income tax–related purposes, need only be kept for the current year. Financial institutions usually print their policy regarding the accuracy of the information somewhere on the statement. An exception to this "current year" rule might be a child's first bankbook, which some people might want to tuck away under "Memorabilia" in the Permanent Files as a keepsake for sentimental reasons.

In general, once credit card statements and associated payments have been verified, there is no reason to keep them. A reasonable practice is to keep them for the current and previous year, then pitch them when you annually purge the files. If you need the information on statements for income tax purposes, then put the relevant ones under "Tax: Income."

There is really no need to keep employment check stubs if your employer issues you the proper documentation needed for income tax purposes. However, if you work for a company but are not deemed to be an employee, then you might want to keep check stubs as proof of employment earnings. If this is the case, you might wish to file these with your personal income files under "Tax: Income." Many people like to keep employment check stubs for the current year to provide an interim financial record until they have received proper year-end documentation from their employer and verified that it is accurate. This is especially important for people whose work hours vary from pay period to pay period. Sometimes employment check stubs are requested by a business or financial institution as proof of income when applying for financial assistance, such as a mortgage or a car loan.

Mortgage documents, personal loan papers and related correspondence need to be kept only until the debt has been repaid or discharged. Some people like to keep the final mortgage or discharge papers showing their home is owned outright; others like to burn them at a party celebrating the fact they are now mortgage-free. Should you ever need proof of your loan history and prompt payment, the original lending institution should have a record of this.

Information and correspondence concerning pension plans should be considered permanent, although you might wish to discard financial statements as they are superseded by more current information.

| | |
|---|---|
| Your financial files may not "match" what a credit agency says about you. Compare your records to theirs to ensure they match. It's a good idea to file a copy of their document with your own records for reference. You can also ask the credit agency to add to your credit record the fact that you have discharged a debt in a timely manner or ahead of schedule. | **Tip: Know Your Credit Rating** |

### Health

Keep here correspondence, documents and records related to health care. In many instances your health care providers will keep most of these records for you. However, if you do have a lot of documentation for specific family members, consider breaking down the files by individual name, for example, "Medical: Adult # 1."

Medical, dental, eye care and other documents related to health care are, for the most part, part of your permanent medical history. You might want to keep only about two years' worth of information with the

Household Files, then transfer the rest into the
Permanent Files under "Health Records."

| | | |
|---|---|---|
| Dental: | General | *Current year plus one; selectively retain* |
| Eye Care: | General | *Current year plus one; selectively retain* |
| Medical: | General | *Current year plus one; selectively retain* |
| Vaccinations | | *Permanent* |

Your doctor, dentist or other health care providers will
likely keep your medical history with their office files
and should it be necessary, your health records should
be available there. Be aware, however, that many offices
have a practice of destroying "inactive files"—files that
have not been used for a long period of time. Check
with your health care providers about their policy.
Make sure that when you move or change health care
providers, your medical records are transferred to the
new caregiver. Note: any receipts needed for income tax
purposes should be filed under "Tax: Income."

**Home**

Keep here documents related to the house structure, its
upkeep and household contents. (In some cases it may
be more appropriate to keep documents related to your
personal property and inventory with your insurance
information.) Mortgage information should be filed
under "Finances," and insurance and tax information
filed under "Insurance" and "Tax," respectively.

| | | |
|---|---|---|
| Assessment | | *Until superseded* |
| Lease | | *Duration of lease* |
| Personal Property/Inventory | | *Until updated* |
| Renovation: | Memorabilia | *Selectively retain* |
| | Permits | *Until final inspection* |
| | Plans | *Selectively retain* |
| | Receipts | *Selectively retain* |
| Repairs: | Major | *Permanent* |
| | Minor | *Current year plus one* |

You will want to transfer receipts or plans that detail major structural changes to your home to your Permanent Files. This is not only for your own reference and ongoing household maintenance, but also to show prospective buyers your home's history and that it has been maintained in good working order. Taxation and assessment information is always available at your city or municipal hall. Personal property and inventory records should be updated periodically and obsolete information thrown out. Consider transferring original documents to the Permanent Files once a year. If you lease your home, you will want to keep a copy of the current lease and related correspondence.

With a major renovation, once the building has been completed and all the final inspections done, you will probably want to keep the documentation only for warranty information, for reference or for sentimental reasons. Revised site plans, surveys and copies of inspections should all be on file with your local governing body (for example, city hall) and should be available to you if ever needed. Receipts, if not necessary for warranty purposes, can be destroyed (after the final tally, if you are not faint of heart, has been calculated!).

## Insurance

Keep here insurance policies and policy information, except as required by law or common practice. (Automobile insurance papers are usually kept with the vehicle.) Also consider keeping a copy only of policies here and keeping the originals off-site in a safety deposit box.

| Policies: | | |
|---|---|---|
| | Automobile | *Until expired* |
| | Boat | *Until expired* |
| | Health | *Until expired* |
| | House | *Until expired* |
| | Life | *Until expired* |

Insurance policies and policy information only benefit you if they are current and the coverage is still valid. There is no need to hang on to expired documentation. Toss it out. Records related to any claims should be kept until the claim has been settled.

## Investments

Keep here correspondence and documents related to personal investments.

| | |
|---|---|
| Annuities | *Until cashed in plus six years* |
| Retirement Savings/Investment Plans | *Current year; permanent* |
| Stocks | *Until cashed in plus six years* |

Correspondence and statements regarding such items as annuities, retirement savings and stocks need to be kept until the investments have been cashed in and all related personal income tax business has been completed. Income tax–related documents can then be filed with "Taxes: Income" and later transferred to the Permanent Files.

## Memberships

Keep here information about organizations of which you are a member.

| | |
|---|---|
| Cultural Institution/Organization | *Current year only* |
| Professional Association | *Current year only* |

You need keep only current information and membership applications. If you wish to keep any documents for sentimental reasons or as memorabilia, refile them once they are no longer needed under "Family and Friends: Memorabilia." Keep in mind that organizations that send you information probably keep copies of it for their records and archives. Check with them if you want to see a copy of a document that was originally produced by them.

## Pets

Keep here correspondence, information and medical records about family pets.

| | |
|---|---|
| Cat (or Pet Name) | *Selectively retain* |
| Dog (or Pet Name) | *Selectively retain* |

Routine information about your family pet (or pets) need only be kept for the current year or until it has expired. This includes information about the annual dog licence, the licence number and information sent to owners at licensing time. Everything else regarding your pet should be kept as long as you own your animal. This includes registration, veterinarian and vaccination records.

### Subscriptions

Keep here correspondence and information about publications to which you subscribe.

| | |
|---|---|
| Magazines | *Until expired* |
| Newspapers | *Until expired* |

As with other contracts, subscription information is only useful to you as long as it is valid. There is no point to keeping outdated subscription information and associated correspondence.

| | |
|---|---|
| **Tip:** **Newspapers** **and** **Magazines** | Read newspapers and magazines and then send them on their way. Either recycle them or donate them to organizations that want them (such as schools, shelters or hospitals). If you must keep magazines, organize them in magazine cartons (available at stationery stores) and then store the cartons in a cupboard or on a bookshelf. |

### Tax

Keep here documents and correspondence related to personal taxes, including income and property tax. Consider transferring documents that must be kept, by law, for a relatively long period of time to the Permanent Files, for example, under "Tax: Income (Year)."

| Income: Personal (United States) | *Three years* |
|---|---|
| Personal (Canada) | *Current year plus six years* |
| Property | *Current year only* |

You will want to keep in your files any receipts or documents to do with personal income tax. Keep your personal income tax files with the Household Files for the current and previous year. This is to ensure that when you go to get the file at tax time, a complete year's worth of information is there, ready for use.

In the United States, authorities at the Internal Revenue Service recommend that individuals keep records such as receipts, canceled checks and other documents proving an item of income or a deduction on a tax return until the statute of limitations expires for that return. Generally, this will be for three years. However, there are other periods specified for certain circumstances, and authorities recommend that individuals keep some records indefinitely, such as property records, since these may be needed to document the amount of gain or loss if the property is sold. A detailed discussion of the various types of basic and specific taxation records, including how long to keep records, is available in the IRS Publication 552, "Recordkeeping for Individuals."

In Canada, taxation laws require you to keep your return for six years, not from the date you mailed it (or from the April 30 tax return deadline), but from the date of final assessment by the Canada Revenue Agency. To comply with this, we suggest you keep your return and all related documentation and receipts for the current year "plus six," hence the benchmark time frame of seven years. (Provided, of course, you file your returns

during the correct taxation year!) Older files that you
do not need immediate access to should be transferred
to the Permanent Files.

## Travel

Keep here information related to travel-point plans or
upcoming vacations.

| | | |
|---|---|---|
| Points/Award Programs: | General | *Current year only* |
| Vacations: | General | *Until no longer needed* |

If you belong to a program or club that involves collecting points to be redeemed for travel, services or merchandise, you are probably only interested to know how
many points you have and information about current
redemption offers. Keep only the latest information. If
for some reason you need information from a newsletter or statement that you have already thrown away,
contact the organization responsible for the program.
They will no doubt have a copy of the information in
their files or archives.

If you are collecting information and schedules for
an upcoming vacation, you'll want to keep the information until it is no longer needed, that is, until the vacation has been taken, your plans have been cancelled or
the information is outdated and no longer valid.
Information about destinations you'd like to visit
should be filed in the Reference Files under "Travel."

## Utilities

Keep here statements, licences and other papers relating to household utilities.

| | | |
|---|---|---|
| Cable | | *Current year plus one* |
| Electricity | | *Current year plus one* |
| Gas | | *Current year plus one* |
| Telephone: | cellular/mobile | *Current year plus one* |
| | local | *Current year plus one* |
| | long distance | *Current year plus one* |
| Water and Sewer | | *Current year plus one* |

Statements and correspondence regarding utilities such as cable, electricity, gas, telephone, water or sewer need only be kept for the current year, unless you need the information for filing income tax deductions. In this case, keep documents for both the current and previous year to ensure you have all necessary information handy at income tax time.

Often copies of statements can be obtained, although usually for a fee, from the utility company. You will save yourself the time and fees associated with obtaining documentation from the originating source by keeping statements for the current year "plus one." Any statements that are used to document income tax claims should then be kept in the Permanent Files under "Tax: Income (Year)."

You might want to keep information pertaining to a major expense or repair for seven to ten years. One telephone company suggested a seven-year time period would be adequate, since the company destroys their records regarding major repairs after seven years.

| **Tip: Double-Duty File Folders** | Many people like to keep information about utility consumption and expenses for interest's sake or budgeting purposes. Rather than keeping all the paper documentation, jotting down notes on the inside of the file folder may allow you to compare statistics from year to year. |
|---|---|

### Warranties and Instructions

Keep here correspondence, warranty information and instructions for currently owned products or services. Note: you could also keep information about how to use items separately in the Reference Files under "Instructions."

| | |
|---|---|
| Appliances | *Until expired or no longer owned* |
| Garden/Outdoor Equipment | *Until expired or no longer owned* |
| Household Furnishings/Products | *Until expired or no longer owned* |
| Household Services/Repairs | *Until expired or no longer owned* |
| Sporting Equipment | *Until expired or no longer owned* |
| Toys and Games | *Until expired or no longer owned* |
| Workshop Equipment and Tools | *Until expired or no longer owned* |

Keep correspondence, warranties and instructions for *only* currently owned products and services. (If you plan to sell or give away products, remember that they have more value if their instructions are still attached.) Go through your files annually and pitch information about products no longer owned or services no longer subscribed to. Once a warranty has expired, it usually serves no purpose. Toss it out.

# Permanent Files

As the name suggests, the documents contained in these files are more or less permanent in nature. These are the documents that are used to establish your identity, ownership and achievements; to provide personal directives (such as the information contained in a will and custody paper); or to document the history of your family.

Items such as birth, marriage and divorce certificates, military papers, religious papers, diplomas and transcripts, as well as social security/insurance cards, are permanent and should be kept for the duration of your life. Other documents, such as passports and personal property records, will change over the years. However, their value in establishing identity and ownership is very important, and these documents should also be regarded as permanent in nature. Personal property records may contain irreplaceable photographs, authentication records, or transaction and purchase receipts that may be difficult to replace as the years tick by.

Permanent files are important because of who they are about. Practice has shown that people are more likely to search permanent files by a person's name than by the form or type of record. By all means use the categories listed, but you might prefer to preface each category by the name of the person (for example, "Mary: Certificates;" "Mary: Education Records").

### Certificates
*Permanent*

Keep here all certificates that establish identity and status, such as birth, death and marriage certificates. Items such as a birth or marriage certificate are used to establish identity and should be kept for the duration of your life.

### Citizenship/Immigration Records
*Permanent*

Keep here any documentation pertaining to citizenship and immigration. Documents pertaining to citizenship and immigration are necessary to keep because they establish identity and rights.

### Divorce Decree/Custody Agreements
*Permanent*

Keep here divorce decrees and documentation that outlines custody agreements or directives. These are legal documents that should form part of a family's permanent record.

### Education Records
*Permanent*

Keep here documents that establish educational achievements. Papers such as graduation certificates or records of marks establish achievements and provide proof of educational accomplishments. You could also keep here samples of schoolwork to document personal history and accomplishment.

## Health Records

*Permanent*

Keep here correspondence, documents and records related to health matters that are not retained by your health care providers. Be familiar with the records retention policies of your health care providers and ensure that you retain significant information if they do not. If you have a large amount of information, subdivide it by the names of your family members and file separately.

## Memorabilia/Family Archives

*Selectively retain*

Keep here any documents that you want to retain for sentimental or genealogical purposes. You can also keep here any records that document the history of your family. What you decide to keep here and for how long is purely a personal choice. But as one archivist has said, keep only the "gold." If space becomes a problem, you can do one of two things. From time to time you could go through this file and reaffirm your decisions about what you are keeping. You might decide to turf some of the memorabilia as new items are added. Or you could transfer information into another area of your home and set it aside in a special area for the family archives. Ideally, this area should be in the main living quarters of your home. Do not store these documents in damp basements or dry attics, where temperature and humidity variations can rapidly destroy your treasures. Keep in mind that any treasures worth keeping are probably worth the time, effort and expense of storing them within archival-quality folders and containers.

### Military Records
*Permanent*

Keep here documents about military service to provide information for pensions, proof of service and family history.

### Personal Property/Inventory Records
*Until superseded*

Keep here documents, including original receipts, photographs or videos, that provide proof of ownership of personal property. Also keep here a listing of household contents. Documents such as personal property records will change over the years. However, they have value in establishing ownership and thus should be regarded as permanent in nature.

### Property Records
*Until no longer owned*

Keep here documents, such as deeds, relating to property you own. As long as you own the property, you will want to keep all documents that establish your ownership rights. Even after you sell property, you might want to selectively retain documents for posterity.

### Religious Documents
*Permanent*

Keep here documents that establish identity, personal history and achievement. These records are viewed by most people to be permanent records that should be kept for the duration of your life. Baptism certificates, confirmation certificates and the like could be required in the event of application for work in a religious institution or for attendance in a religious school.

## Social Security/Social Insurance Documents
*Permanent*

Keep here social security or social insurance information, including original cards. Social insurance number cards are necessary to establish your identity for employment and income purposes (income tax, employment insurance and pension plan benefits).

## Tax Documents
Keep here tax documents for both personal income and any property that you own.

| | |
|---|---|
| Income: Personal (United States) | Three years |
| Personal (Canada) | Current year plus six |
| Property | Selectively retain |

Income tax returns and associated documentation do not have to be kept permanently. However, because the law requires income tax documentation to be kept for a relatively long period of time, it is appropriate to transfer them from the Household Files to the Permanent Files. You do not have to keep property tax records after you have paid the tax, but you might want to keep these records permanently for your own interest, or to document the increases/decreases in value of your home.

## Travel Documents

*Until expired*

Keep here current copies of passports, visas or other travel documents. These documents will change over the years. However, their value in establishing identity is very important, and these documents should be regarded as permanent in nature. Once a travel document has expired and been replaced by current documentation, there is no need to keep outdated information. However, you might want to transfer outdated documents to the Permanent Files under "Memorabilia/ Family Archives."

## Voter Identification Cards

*Until superseded*

Keep here documents used to vote in elections. Voter identification cards are used to establish your identity and eligibility to vote.

## Wills

*Permanent*

We assume original wills are retained off-site for safekeeping. So, keep here current copies of wills—yours and those given to you by family members for information purposes. Personal directives, such as a will, outlining your wishes for the care of yourself and family members or personal property in the event of tragedy or incapacitation should be considered permanent. Only current directives should be kept; destroy all others as soon as new directives are properly drafted and finalized.

Inform your executor of the location of your will and provide them with a photocopy. Review your will and directives
every year, when you go through your file on an annual
purge. If changes are necessary, make proper arrangements
and inform your executor or power of attorney.

**Tip:
Keep Your
Executor
Informed**

## Reference Files

Since reference files contain information of interest to
you but not crucial to the running of your household or
for establishing personal identity, ownership and directives, you really need to ask yourself why you want to
keep information in this category. Often it is because
you think you'd like to refer to the information at some
point "down the road." For example, you'd like to redo
the master bathroom at some point, so you're collecting
decorating ideas from magazines. Or you've clipped an
article from the local paper called "Easy Hikes for
Families" because it might provide some good ideas
when a family member says, "What should we do today?"
But if you do want to keep this information, how long
should you keep it? This kind of information can—and
does—go out-of-date. And if you haven't used the filed
information after a two-year period, what are the chances
that you will refer to it in the future? Get rid of it!

| | |
|---|---|
| Books (to read, reviews, suggestions) | *Current year plus one* |
| Calendars/Course Information | *Current* |
| Catalogs (mail-order, retail) | *Current* |
| Computers:  General Information (and tips) | *Current year plus one* |
| Internet Information (and tips) | *Current year plus one* |
| Crafts (ideas and patterns) | *Current year plus one* |
| Entertainment (party ideas, restaurants, theaters) | *Current year plus one* |
| Garden (ideas) | *Current year plus one* |
| Gift Ideas (by name, by occasion) | *Current year plus one* |
| Instructions (appliances, games, toys) | *Until no longer owned* |
| Parenting (articles) | *Current year plus one* |
| Recipes | *Current year plus one* |
| Travel (ideas, maps) | *Current year plus one* |

You and the members of your household should establish an appropriate time limit for keeping information.
If setting a limit makes you nervous, remember that a
lot of the information you are keeping is available from
the originating source or the library. With electronic
search techniques readily available, searching newspaper and magazine indexes for information is usually
quick and easy. Ask a librarian for help with the procedures.

As with most rules, there are exceptions to setting
specific time limits. One might be for the instructions to
products or services. Maybe you don't play a particular
board game often, but as long as you're keeping the
game, you should probably keep the instructions. The
same is true for instructions about furniture assembly.
Maybe you don't plan to move in the near future, but
when you do, you'll want the instructions on how to
take apart and then reassemble that rolltop desk that

doesn't fit through the door in one piece. In such cases, keep the relevant documentation for as long as you own the furnishings or products—maybe moving them into the Household Files. You might want to also keep instructions for appliances in the Household Files under "Warranties and Instructions." But in general, don't hesitate to toss out information you keep in the Reference Files.

# 4
# What About Electronic Records?

*Organizing, Saving and*
*Preserving Digital*
*Information*

MANY PEOPLE USE A COMPUTER IN SOME CAPACITY TO CREATE, receive or store household information. You may be shopping or paying bills on-line, corresponding with businesses and friends using e-mail, or renewing library books through an on-line catalog. Perhaps you also use a digital camera to produce family photographs in digital format. All of these activities leave us having to cope with electronic records. By *electronic records*, we mean the information you create, receive and store on your computer, including text, data and image files, electronic mail and information downloaded from the Internet. Here's what we've learned (sometimes the hard way!) about managing electronic records, along with some tips and advice.

First the good news: how you deal with your electronic files or photographs should be no different than the way you cope with paperwork. When it comes time to store and find information again, format doesn't matter as much as subject or function. Regardless of format, later on you will want to find these individual files, which may also include information you want to preserve for your family to use and enjoy in the future.

Now the bad news: when it comes to computer technology, it is too easy sometimes to lose valuable information, either accidentally through a system crash or failure, or through the obsolescence of systems and software. Do you have a collection of storage disks that you can no longer read with your computer? Have you ever saved information on disk, then accidentally left the disks on a sunny windowsill, only to have them be unreadable the next day? Have you ever upgraded a software program, then discovered that you can no longer access saved information? Or have you ever selected a software program that disappears from the market, leaving you with no upgrading capability or technical support (what's known as an *orphan system*) or, worse, no compatibility with other systems?

Most of us have lived through the changing formats of recorded music (from vinyl records through eight-track tapes, reel-to-reel tapes and audiocassettes to compact discs) and remember how treasured forms were made useless when all of the technology around them changed. This same change occurs with computers, and if you are creating or saving information of long-term value, you will want to keep the example of recorded music in mind. When you are working with computer records, you need consistent strategies for filing your electronic files and folders, protecting electronic formats and insuring your records against technological obsolescence.

## Naming Files and Directories

A single computer document is usually called a *file*. When working in almost any software program, you will create and save or "save as" a number of related computer files in a *folder*. The folders are usually arrayed in a *directory*, which is like a larger folder or a file drawer. The most important rule in managing computer records is to be consistent in how you name your files and folders.

Thinking back to our discussion of paper records in chapter 2, the logic behind file names and categories is that they are based on the subject of the documents. The same principle applies here: name your individual files with a meaningful title based on the subject of the document. As with your paper files, you will find your computer documents more readily if you have been consistent in naming them and saving or storing them in a logical place.

In the recent past, most software programs limited the size of the name you could apply, which sometimes made it hard to give files a meaningful name. You may still be working with software that has this built-in limitation. However, most programs now have sufficient space to allow you to use the exact title or subject you want, written out in full. This capability makes the file-naming task much easier.

Just as when dealing with paper documents, start by creating an index or directory using our four broad categories: Fingertip, Household, Permanent and Reference. Within these, create folders using the same names (if possible) that you have already assigned to your paper file folders. Then create a meaningful name for individual documents. Place them within these folders.

Whether your records are paper or electronic, always use the same logic and filing structure as outlined in chapter 2. The same rules apply as to what to keep, where to put your records, for how long and why (again, format doesn't matter!). In fact, create one master file plan listing all your files together—paper and electronic. Simply put an asterisk or notation on the master list to indicate which folders are located on the computer hard drive rather than in your household filing cabinet. There may be times when your paper file may also have an electronic component, or your electronic file may have some matching paper correspondence in a file folder. For example, your paper file includes the merchant's correspondence and bill to you, while your payment records may be in electronic files in your computer system. Your master filing plan will help you retrieve all needed information regardless of location.

| | |
|---|---|
| **Tip: File Your Photographs Separately** | If you are building an extensive collection of digital photographs, keep the photographs in a separate file directory. You can sort, organize and retain your photos within the photograph utility software. Although you may not need all four filing categories (Fingertip, Household, Permanent and Reference), you will likely have the same "Family and Friends" subjects that you keep in your permanent records, sorted by date and place. When you back up your data, it's easy to copy the photos onto high-density storage disks when they're all in one place. (Most photographs require more storage capacity than regular floppy disks—soon to be obsolete, no doubt!) |

### Protecting Your Information

After determining how to name your files and where to file them on your drive, the next pressing issue is how to protect the information from accidental loss. Information in the electronic domain is fragile, subject to loss due to a careless keystroke. Several years of valuable information can be gone in seconds. Or you could be robbed, and although the loss of computer hardware is serious, the loss of computer files such as the draft of

your first novel, the family history, trip photos or perhaps sensitive personal and financial information can be
devastating. Therefore, it's important to develop a
regular backup plan. No doubt you have been advised
to back up your data. But we all look for shortcuts or
time-savers when we are busy. Often backing up data is
a task set aside to deal with later (and, of course, later
never comes!). But skipping over this step can be a cost-
ly mistake. A regular backup of all your data is critical.

How often you back up your data will depend upon
how frequently you add or create new information. Ask
yourself, "How long will it take me to re-create my
records if they are lost?" If the answer is "Longer than
I have time for" or "This information is irreplaceable,"
then make this backup a priority. Unlike businesses,
where computer staff complete backups on a regular
basis, as a householder, you will have to plan an appropriate time to do this. Usually, you will be able to copy
your information onto a compact disc or other high-
density storage media. If you have your files organized,
you will be able to quickly identify and copy the recent
information.

Most computer users routinely complete a series of
partial backups and a full backup less frequently. You
will know best the right time to conduct a full or partial
backup of your data. Daily or weekly may be too often,
but probably at least once a month is good practice. If
you are building a significant collection of digital
photographs for your family or scanning family history
documents, you will want to complete a backup every
time you add new materials to your collection. These
are likely items you consider permanent and will want
to protect against any loss.

All of this advice applies to data not only from desktop PCs but also from laptops and hand-held devices. We have a tendency to be a bit blasé about portable devices, but they are easily damaged, lost or stolen. If you are compiling an address book or taking photographs with your personal digital assistant (with camera, voice recording and whatever other extra features!), make sure you back it up to your computer or have a disk copy of your information.

For security's sake, keep your backup data in a safe place some distance away from your computer, and preferably off-site. However, do not keep it in your car or another unheated locale, where fluctuations in temperature may cause your data to disappear.

### Guarding against Obsolescence

In the rapidly changing digital domain, nothing seems to change more often than software. There are new program releases, version upgrades, rewrites and superseded programs. Adapting to new software also means that you have to keep your data current. Large corporations are now investing in software designed solely to maintain digital information in a current state. At a personal level, your strategy should be to migrate forward or copy all of your records and photographs into the new software when you upgrade or when you change to a new program. Why? The risk with updating is that you may lose access to the older data. Depending on your programs, you may have to resave older documents using the new software to guarantee that you can still read and use the files. This is particularly important if the electronic copy is your only copy of important information that you want to continue using.

Not only software, but also hardware and storage devices rapidly become obsolete. It was not that long ago that 5¼-inch floppy discs became 3½-inch floppies, which have now been virtually replaced by compact discs and digital audiotape. If you use any kind of computer, you have to keep up-to-date with the changes that are constantly occurring and, when your storage medium changes, copy your older media to the current format. We call this work "digital housekeeping."

| | |
|---|---|
| If you have precious electronic information that you intend to be accessible over time, consider generating a paper copy of the key computer records and filing them with your paper files, or even off-site for safekeeping. This will enable you to retain a permanent or archival copy. | **Tip: Get Peace of Mind with Paper** |

### Managing Scanned Records

With the increasing storage space available on computers, you may be scanning or creating a digital copy of paper records. Many people are now scanning historic family papers to share with family members as well as to preserve wear on precious original documents. Low-cost, high-resolution scanners are now available, and the input of information is as easy as making a photocopy. As long as you are aware of the pros and cons of storing your information in a computerized environment, an all-digital environment may be a suitable option. Just remember that scanned records, in order to be found again, will require the same type of directory or file-naming conventions already described.

## Electronic Mail and Faxes

In some families, e-mail is replacing the conventional letter or note. It's quick and there are no stamps to lick! These electronic messages consist of several parts. In addition to the message body, the e-mail also includes, in the header, data about who sent the message, when, at what time, and it may also include attachments. The entire three-part message may be important to you. Consequently, you may later need to find the message or refer to it.

Don't make the mistake of filing e-mail in an unsorted gigantic "e-mail file," because it will become too large to facilitate finding messages later. Depending upon the software you use, you should establish an in-basket, then electronically file the messages to the same four categories already discussed: Fingertip, Household, Permanent and Reference. Further subdivide each category as you need, according to your master file plan. You probably don't have to be as detailed as with your paper file categories, but will likely still need to tailor subdivisions for individual topics within your Household and Permanent Files to suit your own purposes. For example, if you receive a lot of personal correspondence, you might want to subdivide your "Family and Friends" category into individual names.

One consideration with e-mail messages is to determine where you want to keep an official record of an e-mail transaction or transmittal, especially when it relates to payment of a bill or debt. If the message is important, you might want to print out the message and any attachment, then file the hard copies in your paper files. The printed record should include all three elements of the e-mail message. Good "digital house-keeping" practice would be to delete the electronic message from your computer when the paper copy is your official record.

Your computer system may be capable of sending and receiving faxes. Apply to faxes the same principles you apply to your electronic mail. Remember that each fax message is actually a two-part message: the information that is transmitted or received, and the information about the transmission or receipt, including who sent it, when and at what time. You might want to print out your transmission log each time you use the fax system to transmit or receive important, and often time-sensitive, materials such as employment applications, communications regarding the selling of your home, or perhaps changes to banking directives.

## How Long Should You Keep It?

It's wise to give some thought to the retention of e-mail messages, since your directory of e-mail messages will grow rapidly. It is the content of the message, rather than the format, that governs how long you should keep it. If you undertake electronic commerce (for example, do your banking in your bathrobe—in front of your computer at home, of course), some of your e-mail messages may be part of your financial records or your operational records. Therefore, you need to follow the retention guidelines that you have established for those file groupings. You will have other e-mail messages (including junk e-mail) that are routine messages that can be read and discarded. One suggestion is to add a date (month or year) to the file title to make it easier to go back through your e-mail.

| **Tip:** **Retention** **Guidelines** | Apply your retention schedule equally to records in all formats, including e-mail and all files in computer directories. Remember, you don't have to keep everything forever. At the same time, you don't want to be overzealous with the "delete" key. Financial records especially may be required at a later time. |
|---|---|

## The Internet

Oh, what a tangled Web we've woven! The Internet, with the World Wide Web, has opened up all sorts of possibilities for us, from rapid global communication to e-commerce transactions to uncomplicated dissemination of information. There is a lot of information available about the Internet. Here we raise Internet issues that relate to information management within your household.

First, you should consider the importance of protecting your information. With an Internet connection, your household information may be accessible to hackers. Your Internet connection may be providing an unlocked entrance into your computer, where the information can be corrupted or stolen. So you need to adopt a defensive strategy, which likely would include a *firewall*. A firewall, just as it sounds, is a device that prevents unauthorized access to your computer or system. Talk to your local Internet service provider or technical support person, who should be able to suggest solutions that are best for you.

You also need to protect your information from viruses. You will want to run a program that can scan for viruses before you download anything from outside sources. This scan can detect any virus or unsafe condition that may compromise or damage your system.

### Managing Records from Your Website

You may decide to establish a personal website—a great way to share news and photos. When you consider the factors involved (the subject of many other books and guides), consider also the record-keeping implications associated with your site. Do you want to document what you put on the site? For some people, their website will become another form of the family history. If this describes your situation, then a dated copy of the content of the Web pages will provide an adequate record of what is mounted and maintained. In other words, take periodic "snapshots" of the information, so that a future record is available to you.

| | |
|---|---|
| It's easy for your computer hard drive to become as messy as your paper records, your closet and other visible places where stuff accumulates. Apply the organizing and retention principles to ensure that you can find your "cyber" records when you need them. | **Tip: Avoid Digital Clutter** |

How much you use a computer will ultimately depend upon the nature of your household and your own technology comfort level. Don't overlook the potential benefits of computer applications. But recognize that computers will produce records that, like the paper ones you know and deal with, will require care and preservation for future reference.

# 5
# Under Control
*Maintaining Your*
*Household Filing System*

ONCE YOU'VE GOT YOUR HOUSEHOLD FILING SYSTEM IN PLACE, USE it—and *enjoy it*. Enjoy the newfound serenity you experience when you can find things quickly. But keep in mind that the system must be maintained. It will only be useful if people use it.

Make an effort to use and maintain your household filing system for 21 days. That's how long experts suggest it takes to make something new become part of your regular routine. Think of the 21-day period as a trial run. You can then make changes based on your experience of the system and how it has worked for you during this period.

| | |
|---|---|
| Create an in-box near the information center of your home for kids to use. They can drop any papers from school into it and know that you'll see the information. By the same token, you could create an out-box that everyone in the house checks on their way out the door, picking up videos to return, letters to mail, and so on. | **Tip:** **An In-Box** **for the Kids** |

### The Annual Purge

From time to time, any filing system needs a little maintenance. Set aside some time once a year to tend your files. A good time of year might be spring (after income tax season) or fall (before the school year starts). July could be the ideal time of year. By this month (provided you filed your income tax documents on time), you should have received your final notice of assessment. If everything is in order and you haven't been asked to provide any other documents for income tax purposes, you can probably go ahead and weed your files according to the guidelines you've already established, removing information no longer needed. And this process shouldn't take too long. You've already made decisions about what to keep, for how long and why. Now you simply follow your guidelines to transfer information into another file or toss it out if no longer needed. You can also prepare your summary pages (if you are keeping them) at this time. Set up new or replacement file folders or containers as necessary. Move information that was in the Household Files (but slated to move into the Permanent Files) into the appropriate permanent file categories.

| **Tip:** **A Fun** **Family** **Event** | One person, who was responsible for a family of five, set up this system and found that she was able to weed the Household Files completely in 20 minutes. Okay, 20 minutes not counting the children's schoolwork. That took a little longer, but she found it enjoyable to sit down with each child and go through the schoolwork, deciding which samples were worth keeping. If you want to plan an evening at home, you can get the kids involved in the annual purge. Then they, too, will learn how to use and maintain the household filing system. |

**Curbing and Eliminating Unwanted Information**

Remember, the less information you have, the less you have to organize and maintain. The trick is to eliminate unwanted information in the first place. Remember the principles of the recycling process—"refuse, reduce, reuse, recycle"? Here are some practical ways to curb or eliminate unwanted information.

- If magazines are stacking up unread, think about cancelling subscriptions. Make sure that your newspaper and magazine subscriptions suit your reading patterns and needs.
- Check with the post office for suggestions about ways to curb unwanted mail.
- Check direct marketing association websites for helpful tips and advice on how to remove your contact information from phone, mail and e-mail lists: Direct Marketing Association (U.S.), *www.the-dma.org*; Canadian Marketing Association, *www.the-cma.org*.
- Contact individual companies and ask to be removed from their mailing list.
- When telephone solicitors call you, tell them you want your name removed from their list.
- Think twice about entering "free" draws advertised in magazines and stores. The purpose of these is often to obtain your contact information so that they can market to you by mail or by phone.
- Put an "empty hands and empty pockets" policy into effect. Restrain yourself from picking up free literature or brochures, unless you're really interested in the information.
- Watch out for "Opt In" or "Opt Out" boxes that appear on application forms and use them accordingly. If you "Opt In," your name and

contact information will be placed on (yet) another mailing list.

- Consider carefully decisions to join mail-order clubs (for books, music or crafts). There seems to be a lot of correspondence associated with these clubs and it seems to go on for years.
- Consider getting an unlisted telephone number. A drastic measure, perhaps, but one person tells us that when she switched to an unlisted telephone number, the number of unsolicited telephone calls she received dropped remarkably.
- Remove your name from computer listservs if you seldom bother to read the messages.

## Final Words

We hope you can see that controlling your paperwork is a process. You'll never be "done," but with the tips we've given here and this filing system, you can be in control of the continuous stream of incoming items.

If you've come this far with us, you've already done the hard part of the work. The rest is much easier. Keep your Fingertip Files in order each day (over a cup of tea, perhaps?). Since your Household, Reference, and Permanent Files have all been set up, adding to them will be a simple process, one that is as quick or as leisurely as you like.

Good luck with your records. And again, a reminder that this book deals only with household records. If you need help with your home-based or small-business records, refer to our book *At Your Fingertips in the Office: Information Management for the Small Business*. Further information about our publications and other useful resources is available on our website, *www.streamlinebooks.com*.

# Appendix A: Hands On!

## Setting Up Fingertip Files

There are many way to set up Fingertip Files. You can arrange file folders inside a decorative wicker basket. Maybe you prefer to hang file folders inside a kitchen drawer. Another option is a set of binders that sits on the counter by the telephone and keeps your information right where you need it—at your fingertips. Whatever setup you choose, make sure the look and feel of your files suits you.

In this section we describe one possible setup in detail, using binders and the three categories "Calendar," "Contacts/Schedules/Newsletters" and "Shopping/Family Business." Modify the categories to suit your own system. If you think one binder will suffice, by all means condense the categories into one binder. And, to make the process more manageable, we suggest setting aside one day to gather supplies and another day to tackle the job of setting up the files. If you have Internet access, visit our website, *www.streamlinebooks.com*, to download the binder inserts described below.

### Calendar Binder

You will need the following supplies to set up your *Calendar Binder:*

- a one-inch binder with a clear spine label and pockets on the inside front and inside back cover
- 12 extra-wide tab dividers
- 28 heavy-duty, top-loading sheet protectors
- a current 12-month calendar. Choose a calendar that has a separate sheet for each month of the current

year, then separate it so you have 12 individual sheets. If you have access to a calendar-making software program, you might want to print off 12 monthly calendars.

- 28 8½- x 11-inch sheets of paper
- a glue stick

## Assembly

1. Label your binder "Calendar."
2. Label the 12 tab dividers by month, with one month on each tab, starting with January.
3. Glue a current calendar month onto the front of each appropriate tab divider.
4. Insert the 12 dividers into the binder.
5. Insert 17 sheet protectors behind the current monthly tab divider (that is, the month you are in).
6. Insert one sheet protector behind each of the remaining tab dividers.
7. Take 12 of the 8½- by 11-inch sheets of paper and label them by month (one month for each piece of paper— "January," "February," and so on). Place the sheet marked "January" into the sheet protector behind the tab divider marked "January." Place each remaining sheet into the appropriate sheet protector behind its matching monthly tab divider.
8. Take the remaining 16 8½- by 11-inch sheets of paper. On the first sheet write "Day 1." On the reverse side of the sheet, write "Day 2." On the next sheet write "Day 3" on the front, "Day 4" on the reverse, and so on, until "Day 31." (Note: there will be no writing on the reverse side of the Day 31 sheet). Place the sheets into the sheet protectors behind the current monthly tab divider and first sheet protector, so you have one sheet per sheet protector, starting with Day 1.

## How to Use the Calendar Binder

Use the monthly calendar on each tab divider to jot down appointments, school field trips, dinner dates, etc. Use the sheet protectors (referred to as pockets from now on) to hold information that you might need on a particular day.

For example, say the current month is January. The first thing you should see when you open your *Calendar Binder* is the tab divider with the January calendar on it. Following that should be the pocket labeled "January," followed by pockets for individual calendar days. It's been a busy day . . .

- You buy tickets to the theater for January 21. When you get home, mark the theater date on the calendar. Put the tickets into the pocket marked "Day 21."
- Grandma calls. She knows you usually go grocery shopping on Thursday evenings. She wants you to pick up some toothpaste that is on sale. You see that your next Thursday shopping will be on January 10. Jot yourself a note and stick it in the pocket marked "Day 10."
- Sally brings home a school notice about a field trip to the art gallery and what she needs to bring (for example, a bag lunch) on January 28. Mark the field trip on the calendar. Put the notice into the pocket marked "Day 28."
- Johnny is going on a field trip, too. He's going to the nature park on January 27. The notice he's brought home also has a tear-off permission slip that must be filled out and returned to the school as soon as possible. Fill out the permission slip and put it into the pocket marked with tomorrow's date. Put the other part of the notice into the pocket marked "Day 27."

- You receive an invitation to the opening of the new community center on February 13. Go to the calendar for February and mark the opening on the 13th. Put the invitation into the pocket labeled "February."
- You receive an invitation to a wedding for "March" 17. You decide to go. Send off your reply, then write the wedding onto your calendar for "March." Put the invitation in the pocket labeled March. You decide that you'd like to send a gift ahead of time. Sometime in February is probably a good time to go shopping. Write yourself a note and slip it into the pocket for February.
- You receive a letter from Aunt Mary but can't reply today. You'll probably get a moment to jot her a line on the weekend. Put the letter into the appropriate date. (You could write yourself a note on the calendar if you want, but with this type of item, it's probably fine to simply put it in the pocket for the particular day. When you are reviewing the calendar and checking the pockets, you'll see the letter.)

Tonight before you go to bed, check the calendar and appropriate pocket. If you want to, pull out the contents of tomorrow's pocket and stick it into the inside front cover pocket of the binder, ready for use. Go to bed *confident* that the information you need tomorrow is *at your fingertips*. All the information you need will be there ready for you to use or distribute as appropriate in the morning.

At the end of each day you can simply refile into the appropriate pocket things you didn't deal with during that day (for example, an item on a "to-do" list). Most of the information in these pockets can be tossed as soon as you're done with it. The exception might be a special invitation or tickets that you'd like to save for a scrapbook or memory book. In this case you'd simply transfer the item to an appropriate file in the Household, Permanent or Reference Files.

At the end of the month, move the next calendar month into position before the day pockets and transfer any information from that month's pocket to the appropriate day pockets.

## Contacts/Schedules/Newsletters Binder

You will need the following supplies for the *Contacts/ Schedules/Newsletters Binder:*

- a one-inch binder with a clear spine label and pockets on the inside front and inside back cover
- 12 or more heavy-duty, top-loading sheet protectors
- one or two business cardholder sheets for three-ring binders
- optional: three extra-wide tab dividers labeled "Contacts," "Schedules," "Newsletters"

## Assembly

1. Label your binder "Contacts/Schedules/Newsletters."
2. Insert the business cardholder sheets.
3. Insert the sheet protectors.

## How to Use the Contacts/ Schedules/Newsletters Binder

Use the sheet protectors to hold any contact lists, schedules and newsletters that you keep and use the business cardholder sheets for business cards you keep.

Throw away information once it becomes outdated. For example, discard old school newsletters as soon as you receive the latest copy. If you do want to keep any of this information, don't keep it here. Transfer it into the Household Files or the Permanent Files as appropriate. Here is a list of the information you might want to include in this binder.

- Personal contact sheet
- Business cards
- New numbers to add to phone lists
- List of personal phone numbers and addresses
- School friendship list(s)
- Sports teams phone lists
- Block Watch neighbourhood list
- Telephone banking brochure (phone numbers and how to use the service)
- Post office information (contact numbers and postal rates)
- Library information (phone numbers, opening hours)
- Schedules (garbage/recycling, swimming pools, ferries, buses)
- Newsletters (elementary school, Block Watch, clubs)

**Tip: Don't Forget Your Own Name**

In a busy household, it's a good idea to make the first item in your binder a personal contact sheet giving your name, address, work information and emergency contacts (including 911 and Poison Control). This is really useful to have handy and to leave out for a babysitter, and it's a convenient place to start to teach young children about this information in the event of an emergency. You can put specific information about where you are going in the inside cover pocket of the binder.

**Shopping/Family Business Binder**

You will need the following supplies for the *Shopping/
Family Business Binder:*

- a one-inch binder with a clear spine label and pockets
  on the inside front and inside back cover
- eight to 12 heavy-duty, top-loading sheet protectors
  (add more as necessary)
- eight to 12 8½- by 11-inch sheets of paper

**Assembly**

1. Label your binder "Shopping" (or the name you have
   given this file—it might be something like "Financial
   Transactions").
2. Insert the sheet protectors.
3. Label the 8½- by 11-inch sheets of paper with the
   categories you have decided upon, such as "Receipts for
   Groceries," "Coupons and Offers," "Take-Out Menus,"
   "Credit Card Receipts," "Merchandise Receipts" and
   "Banking Receipts." If you have more than one credit
   card and use credit cards frequently, consider making
   a separate pocket for each credit card, for example,
   "Credit Card Receipts: Name of Company." Similarly,
   you might divide your coupons into more detailed
   categories if you collect and use coupons regularly.

**How to Use the Shopping/Family Business Binder**

Use this binder to keep track of information you collect
or use when shopping—whether it be store sales
announcements and flyers, take-out food menus,
coupons to use at the grocery stores, or sales receipts.
The idea is to keep information handy. When Friday
night rolls around and you decide to order out, you
won't get frustrated digging through the kitchen drawer

or leafing through the dozens of entries in the Yellow Pages—the menus of the restaurants you use (or are likely to use) are all together in your binder. And before you go shopping, you'll be able to quickly locate the relevant coupon.

Keep all your receipts here, too—credit card slips, merchandise receipts that you paid cash for, banking receipts and service receipts. Keep credit card and banking receipts here until your statements arrive. Check the receipts against your statement, then get rid of them (you should probably shred or otherwise destroy them), unless you need to keep a particular receipt for insurance, warranty or income tax purposes. In most cases, once you've verified the statement as correct, there's no need to keep the receipts. File your verified statement in your Household Files under "Finances: Credit Card (Name of Company)." Receipts you want to keep should be transferred from the *Shopping/Family Business Binder* to the appropriate household file, such as "Tax: Income," or to your Permanent Files. It's a good rule of thumb to keep receipts for cash purchases of merchandise until the return policy time period has passed, unless they're needed for some other purpose. If you have pockets for receipts for merchandise, weed them on a regular basis. Other pockets should be weeded each month, or whenever you verify your financial statements.

### The Shopping/Family Business Binder in Action—An Example

You've been on a shopping spree . . .

First you stopped at the bank machine to withdraw $100. Then you stopped at the bakery (and spent $5), and at the vegetable market (and spent $7.50). You knew you probably shouldn't, but the bookstore is one of your favorite haunts; you stopped there. (Fifty-six dollars went onto your credit card.) Then it was off to the electronics shop for a new VCR (again, on the credit card). You passed a really great children's clothing store and bought a birthday present for your two-year-old nephew (and paid in cash). Finally you get home, tired, happy, and ready for a final treat—a take-out supper. But first, you empty your wallet and shopping bags of all your receipts. Where do they go?

The bank receipt goes into the pocket marked "Banking Receipts." It will stay there until the bank statement arrives, at which time you will verify the statement with all your banking transaction receipts. If all is correct, you'll go ahead and shred the receipts.

The bakery and vegetable market cash receipts can get tossed right away. No need to keep them unless you use them for budgeting purposes.

The credit card slips from the bookstore and the electronics shop go into the pocket marked "Credit Card Receipts." Those receipts will stay there until the credit card statement arrives, at which time you will verify the receipts against the statement. Unless you returned any of the items you purchased, once the statement has been verified, it's time to send the receipts on their way.

The bookstore receipt can probably be shredded, but the electronics shop receipt (which provides details on the VCR that you might need for warranty or insurance purposes) should be put in the pocket marked "Merchandise Receipts," and then moved to the Household Files under "Home: Personal Property." The receipt for your nephew's gift also goes into the pocket marked

"Merchandise Receipts." That's where it will be if you need to exchange the item for something in a larger size.

At last, the details are out of the way and it's time to order supper. You flip to the pocket in your binder marked "Take-Out Menus" to find the telephone number of one of your favorite spots.

| Tip:<br>For<br>Coupon<br>Collectors | Consider using photo album inserts to hold your various coupons. The inserts with pockets for four-by-six-inch photos are ideal for visibility and keep the sorting of your coupons easy. |
| --- | --- |

## Setting Up Household Files

Here are some suggestions for quickly setting up your Household Files. You will need to buy some file folders, preferably letter-size, in a top-tab style for storage in a drawer or box, or in a side-tab style for storage on a shelf. You might also want to have labels on which to type or write your file names. If you selected categories from "The Household Filing System at a Glance," you'll need 15 to 20 folders.

### Assembly

1. From the list of file subjects in this book, select the subjects that describe your files. (See page 16 for a list of suggested subjects and chapter 3 for further breakdowns.) Mark the selected subjects with a highlighter pen or make your own list.

2. Prepare a file folder for each subject required and label each folder on its tab.

3. Sort your household papers into the selected subjects as you sort. If you have a lot of paper to sort through and organize, you might want to write the subject (in pencil) on each document to be filed.

4. File the documents into the file folders, placing them in date order (oldest documents on the bottom, recent documents on top).

5. Arrange the folders in alphabetical order and put them into the drawer, box or container (or the onto the shelf) you've selected as the home for these records.

**How to Use the Household Files**

On a regular basis, add information from the Fingertip Files and incoming mail into the Household Files. On an annual basis, review your system, remove unneeded records and move records into the Permanent Files.

# Appendix B: Resources
*Further Help in Getting Organized*

## Websites

Our own websites, *www.streamlinebooks.com* and *www.harwoodinformation.com,* offer publications, stories, tips and supplies. In addition, the following are expert sources to check if you need further information.

### Taxation Authorities
Internal Revenue Service, United States
www.irs.gov

Canada Revenue Agency
www.ccra-adrc.gc.ca

### Professional Associations
Association of Records Managers and Administrators (ARMA International), United States and Canada
www.arma.org

Society of American Archivists (SAA), United States
www.archivists.org

Association of Canadian Archivists
www.archivists.ca

**Professional  Organizing Services and Resources**

National Association of Professional Organizers
(NAPO), United States and Canada
www.napo.net

Professional Organizers in Canada
www.organizersincanada.com/

123 Sort it
http://123sortit.com

Organized Forever
www.organizedforever.com

**Photograph Management**

OrganizedPhotos.com, United States and Canada
www.OrganizedPhotos.com

## Our Favorite Suppliers

The Container Store, United States
www.containerstore.com

Family Jewels Archival Preservation Co.,
United States and Canada
www.familyjewelsarchival.com

Hold Everything, United States
www.holdeverything.com

IKEA, worldwide
www.ikea.com

Office Depot, United States and Canada
www.officedepot.com

Staples/Business Depot, United States and Canada
www.businessdepot.com

## Publications

Don't let the publication dates fool you—these are all really great books. At time of printing, all except the *Digital Photograph Pocket Guide* were available through amazon.com.

Bradley, Alexandra, and Denise Dale. (2000). *At Your Fingertips in the Office: Information Management for the Small Business.* Streamline Information and Organizing Services. ISBN 0968572715

Braun, Bev Kirschner. (2000). *Crafting Your Own Heritage Album.* Betterway Publications. ISBN 1558705341

Fulton, Alice, and Pauline Hatch. (1991). *It's Here . . . Somewhere.* Rev. ed. Writers Digest Books. ISBN 0898794471

Kingston, Karen. (1999). *Clear Your Clutter with Feng Shui.* Broadway. ISBN 0767903595

Lehmkuhl, Dorothy, and Dolores Cotter Lamping. (1993). *Organizing for the Creative Person: Right Brain Styles for Conquering Clutter, Mastering Time, and Reaching Your Goals.* Three Rivers Press. ISBN 0517881640

Long, Jane S., and Richard W. Long. (2000). *Caring for Your Family Treasures: Heritage Preservation.* Harry N. Abrams. ISBN 0810929090

Smallin, Donna. (2002). *Organizing Plain and Simple: A Ready Reference Guide with Hundreds of Solutions to Your Everyday Clutter Challenges.* Storey Books. ISBN 1580174485

Storey, Derrick. (2002). *Digital Photograph Pocket Guide.* O'Reilly and Associates. ISBN 0596004540

# Acknowledgments

IN WRITING OUR BOOKS, WE HAVE EACH TAKEN A DIRECTION away from our expected careers and into another set of work experiences entirely different from our library and office lives. Denise was a student of Sandie's, and her need for a household filing system to keep a home renovation, university education and three small children organized was the foundation for our record-keeping system in *At Your Fingertips! A Household Filing System That Works for You*. As we toured bookstores and shared our ideas with readers, we quickly discovered that a lot of people were looking for specific advice about their small-business records. Full of enthusiasm, we completed *At Your Fingertips in the Office: Information Management for the Small Business*. Small-business owners everywhere are finding it a useful guide, and it is even being used as a business textbook.

With this second edition of our first book, the advice expands to help householders address the sometimes perplexing, sometimes frustrating issues surrounding computer records. Our readers (and booksellers and interviewers) continue to share their records- and information-management stories with us. There seems to be no end to the stories, and we now find that with an emphasis on "getting rid of the clutter," many of the lifestyle issues people face include a records management dilemma.

We are heartened by the endorsements we continue to receive from our peers in the library and records-management communities. And, without a doubt, our families and our friends are our best advocates, our best marketers and enduring supporters in our writing adventures.

Our editor, Naomi Pauls, of Paper Trail Publishing, has been with us from the beginning of our first book. She continues to be our best critic and brings out our best efforts because, as her motto says, print matters. Our thanks extend to the designers who worked on various editions of our books, Rick Carty and Leon Phillips, and to Meisner Publicity and Promotion.

*Sandie Bradley*
*Denise Dale*
*March 2004*

# Index

# Notes

If you need additional copies of this book, please look for it at your local bookstore or contact the publisher at:

**Streamline Information and Organizing Services**
186 – 8210 No. 2 Road, Suite #271
Richmond, British Columbia
Canada  V7C 2V4
www.streamlinebooks.com